13.95

SCIENCE FAIR
HOW TO DO A SUCCESSFUL PROJECT

MICROBES

BY
JOHN M. LAMMERT

SERIES CONSULTANT
DR. JOHN M. LAMMERT
Associate Professor of Biology
Gustavus Adolphus College
St. Peter, Minnesota

**ROURKE
PUBLICATIONS
INC.**
Vero Beach, FL 32964
U.S.A.

LIBRARY OF CONGRESS CATALOGUING-IN-PUBLICATION DATA

Lammert, John, 1943–
    Microbes / by John M. Lammert
        p. cm.
    Summary: Explains the scientific method and suggests projects and
experiments about microbes suitable for a science fair.
    ISBN 0-86625-430-7
    1. Microbiology—Juvenile literature. 2. Science projects—Juvenile literature.
[1. Microbiology—Experiments. 2. Experiments. 3. Science projects.]
I. Title II. Series.
QR57.L34 1992
576' .078—dc20
                                                            92-9123
                                                            CIP
                                                            AC

DESIGNED & PRODUCED BY:
MARK E. AHLSTROM
(The Bookworks)

PHOTOGRAPHY:
Cover–THE IMAGE BANK/Alfred Pasieka
Text–MARK E. AHLSTROM

TABLE OF CONTENTS

CHAPTER 1

What Makes A Science Project "Scientific?"

In a good science project, you will be an investigator. You will look at clues provided by the world about you and will make some sense of them by planning and doing an experiment. This is what scientists do when they observe some natural phenomenon and want to investigate it—they use the **scientific method**. In an organized fashion, scientists follow a series of steps that are designed to help them come up with an explanation for something they have observed.

When scientists observe something new, they wonder "How can that be?" The scientists have identified a problem. A scientist then makes an educated guess, or a **hypothesis**, that might explain the observation or solve the problem. It is "educated" because the scientist has some knowledge of the subject matter or reads what other scientists have found out through their experiments about the problem.

Steps Followed in the Scientific Method

✔ Make an *observation*.

✔ State the problem: What do you want to find out?

✔ What is already known about the observation?

✔ Develop a *hypothesis*: What do you think is a reasonable explanation for the observation?

✔ Design an *experiment* that will provide answers: What materials will be needed and how will they be used?

✔ Record *data* or observations: What happened during the experiment?

✔ Analyze the results.

✔ Come to a *conclusion*: What did you learn? Did your data support your hypothesis? What do your results mean?

Let's look at an example of an observation. From this observation, a hypothesis will be made.

You see that the wood around a window is rotting away. The paint has started to peel away. The wood looks black and crumbles when you push on it. Then, you look at an old wooden fence post sticking out of the ground. You push on it a little bit, but the post doesn't break. After you dig away some of the dirt where the post enters the ground, you see that very little wood has rotted away. You remember reading in a book that rotting, or decay, is a natural process. Material that was once part of a living creature (called **organic** material) is broken down by very small living things called **microbes**. Many microbes use organic matter for food. A good question about wood and rotting might be "Do some types of wood rot more rapidly than others do?" You might then make the hypothesis, or prediction, that "Some types of wood rot faster than others do."

Someday this rotten window may fall out.

Next, the scientist makes a plan to test the hypothesis. This plan is called the **experimental design**. Materials are chosen and a series of steps are written out. Then the actual work can start.

Here is an experimental design for our hypothesis that some kinds

5

of wood rot faster than others. In this experiment, small pieces of different woods will be placed in soil. These wood pieces have been weighed before they are stuck in the soil. After seven weeks, the wood pieces will be taken out of the soil, brushed off, and weighed again. How much wood material has been lost because of rotting will then be calculated.

Then the actual work can start. Three kinds of wood are chosen: pine, redwood, and fir. Four small blocks of each wood are cut. The dimensions of each wood block are 4.0 **centimeters** (cm) long and 1.25 cm square. The wood blocks are dried for a week. An identification number is marked near one end of each dried wood piece. They are each weighed to the nearest 0.1 **gram** (g). The weights are recorded in

Wood pieces are put in baby jars with soil.

a lab notebook. Three baby food jars are half-filled with moist (not soaking wet) soil from a garden or a woods. Potting soil purchased from a garden supply center is not used because it has been **sterilized,** or treated to kill all microbes in it. Three pieces of each wood type are stuck halfway into the soil of one baby food jar. Each jar is marked to identify the type of wood in it.

Another jar has no soil in it. One block of each wood type is placed in this jar. This jar is called a **control** because soil to rot the wood is missing. The lids are loosely placed on the jars to let air get in. The jars are then kept in a dark warm corner for seven weeks. They are checked daily to see if anything is happening. If the soil looks dry, a little bit of water is added. However, the same amount of water is added to the three jars that contain soil.

During the experiment **data** are collected. This means that what you see or what you measure is recorded. In our example, the amount of wood rotted away by microbes in the soil will be measured. When seven weeks are over, the wood blocks are taken out and the soil is scraped off. The control blocks are also removed from their jar. All pieces are dried for one week. The blocks are again weighed to the nearest 0.1 g.

The **results** are studied. The amount of wood material that has been eaten by soil microbes from each wood sample is calculated as follows:

$$\text{Percentage of wood rotted away} = \frac{(\text{starting weight} - \text{final weight})}{\text{starting weight}} \times 100\%$$

An average percentage is calculated for each kind of wood. The control blocks are also weighed to see if any of their weights were lost.

Finally, from these results, **conclusions** are made. What was learned? Did any type of wood lose more weight than others? Was the hypothesis correct, that is, did the data and the hypothesis agree? If it was not correct, then what would be another hypothesis?

The scientist will then use these data to make some **predictions** that might lead to more experiments. What conditions are needed for wood to rot? Why might some woods rot faster than others? What kinds of wood are best for building things that will be kept outdoors? How can rotting be prevented? What happened to the missing wood? When the data from an experiment have been studied, there are often new questions that require answers. A scientist doesn't stop doing experiments even after winning the Nobel Prize!

A scientist's work is never done.

CHAPTER 2

Choosing Microbes As A Topic For Your Project

What makes a good science project? Students with experience will probably tell you that the hardest part is finding a topic. Take plenty of time trying to think of a good topic. This book is written to help you decide what to do. It's important that you are interested in the topic you choose. This means that you will be excited about what you are doing. You usually learn better when you are excited about something. Don't think you must have a difficult project, especially if this is your first. The best projects often focus on something simple.

The tiny living creatures called **microbes** provide many fascinating features to study. They can be seen growing as green spots on a rotten orange, or as slimy "gook" on a steak that has remained in the refrigerator too long. Some microbes are added to bread dough so that the loaves will rise and be full of holes. Microbes change milk into yogurt and put the holes in Swiss cheese. Microbes help recycle dead stuff. Leaves and dead animals decay in a forest when microbes eat them. Unwashed gym socks smell because of microbes. A few microbes can make you sick. A tooth cavity is started by microbes that eat the sugar from candy and cereal. Others can make your throat sore, give you an upset stomach, or create a rash on your skin. Individual microbes are much too small to see without magnifying them several hundred times in a microscope.

Microbes are all around you and everyplace else. They grow in water, in soil, and on plants and animals. Some grow in the snow and others live in very hot water. They are blown about by the wind. A great number make your body their home. They grow on your skin and thrive on your tongue, teeth, and cheeks, in your nose and throat, and in your intestines.

The living world of microbes includes the **bacteria**, the **molds**, and the **yeasts**. Biologists consider the molds and yeasts to be related to each other. They are part of a group of living things called **fungi** (*fun*

9

JEYE). Bacteria, when they are magnified with a microscope, are seen to come in three basic shapes. Round bacteria are called **cocci** (*COCK zeye*). Rod-shaped bacteria are called **bacilli** (*bah SILL eye*). Other bacteria have a spiral shape. Bacteria are so small that 5000 could be lined up on a pencil eraser.

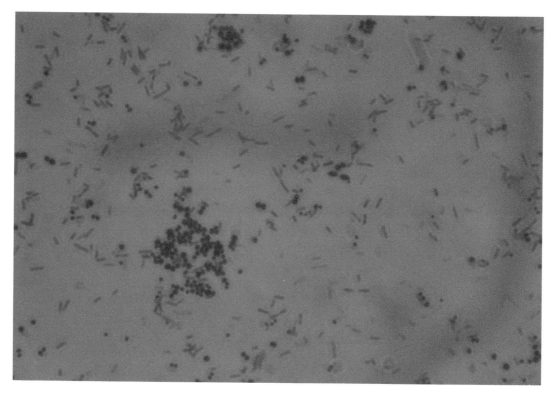

What bacilli and cocci look like in a microscope.

Molds form a fuzzy coat on old bread or rotting oranges. Closer inspection of these green or black coats with a strong magnifying glass shows many threads spreading all over. Rising up from some threads are knob-like structures that contain **spores**. Molds spread themselves by releasing these spores into the air or by sticking to insects. At some point a spore will settle on a new food supply and grow into a new mold. When yeasts are observed through a microscope, they look like eggs.

As living creatures, microbes need to take in and use energy for growth, to obtain food and water, and to produce more of their kind. Some microbes capture light from the sun and use the energy to grow.

Others prefer to grow in the dark. Many microbes feed on **organic** matter, substances made by living things. However, some bacteria have strange appetites and eat things that contain iron or sulfur.

Bacteria make more of their kind by a process called **binary fission**. A single bacterium (*back TEER ee um*) grows bigger in size and then splits into two bacteria that are exactly the same. Each of these bacteria divides into two new bacteria a little later. Now, there are four bacteria. If bacteria are placed in the best temperature and given lots of food, water, and space, many can divide every 30 minutes. This means that after one hour, four bacteria can come from one bacterium. After two hours, there will be 16 bacteria, and after 12 hours, almost 17 million.

Each type of microbe has its own needs. Some microbes can grow in many places, while others are picky about where they live. Temperature affects the growth of microbes. Some like it hot, some like it cold, and some like the temperatures we prefer. Many microbes use oxygen in the air to grow, while others will die if oxygen is present. That is why these tiny creatures can live under our gums, in our intestines, and deep in the ground.

This book will guide you through the basic steps you need to follow to do a successful science project about microbes. In the next few pages you will read about project ideas that focus on microbes. You will not find many step-by-step instructions. Instead, the ideas are here to spark your imagination and to turn on your creative powers. That's what makes science fun—imagination and creativity.

What types of projects can you do about microbes?

There are three different types of projects you can choose to do about microbes:

☆ You can prepare an *exhibit* that displays a collection or shows what you learned after reading about a topic.

☆ You can do a *demonstration* of a lab experiment you found in a book.

☆ You can do an *investigation* that uses the scientific method to explore a problem.

Sometimes, science fair rules discourage the first two types of projects. Teachers or judges may feel that these projects are not scientific enough. However, you might be able to do an exhibit or demonstration *if* you add a little investigation to the project. It's a good idea to have your teacher go over your project plans with you. This will help you find out if your project satisfies your local rules.

☞ *Exhibits*

For centuries, people have used microbes to make food. In a pizza, the crust, cheeses, ripe olives, and pepperoni sausage result from the activities of microbes. Mushrooms are a type of fungus and so they are

Microbes make pizza possible.

big microbes. Other foods that are made because of the activities of microbes include breads, butter, sour cream, yogurt, vinegar, pickles, tofu, and soy sauce. Foods can spoil if they are not stored correctly. Many foods are grown far away from people who will eat the foods. Therefore, steps must be taken by factories to insure that food will not spoil before someone buys it at a supermarket. Food is canned, frozen, and freeze-dried to preserve it. Sometimes people can become sick because food has not been properly handled. You could prepare an exhibit about one of these food topics:

✦ Microbes and making foods
✦ Food poisoning
✦ Microbes and food preservation

Microbes are tiny chemical factories that take raw material from the environment and change it into other things. To a microbe, this might be waste matter. But, to us, it can be useful. Microbes are harnessed to make **antibiotics**, drugs that doctors use to treat infections caused by other microbes. Microbes are also grown to make vitamins, such as vitamin C and riboflavin. The ingredients that are used to make some artificial sweeteners are produced by bacteria. **Enzymes** are substances used by living things to change other substances. Scientists have discovered ways to use enzymes from microbes to make meat tenderizers, stain removers in laundry detergent, sugar in soft drinks, and shoe leather. Have you ever wondered how that soft center got in the middle of chocolate-covered cherries? An enzyme made by certain bacteria is added when the candy is made. Even the flavor of chocolate comes from microbes. An exhibit that presents information on industrial uses of microbes could be prepared.

Waste water must be treated to remove organic matter and harmful microbes. Sewage treatment plants are designed to do this. You could put together a display that shows how sewage is treated in your community.

Viruses are strange microbes. They are so small that several thousand viruses that cause a cold can fit over the period at the end of this sentence. Viruses cannot live on their own. They must invade living cells so they can reproduce. Several hours after a virus has raided a cell, the cell is damaged or may die as dozens of new viruses pop out. These offspring then get into other cells. When this happens inside your body, you can become sick. Viruses cause colds, influenza, measles, mumps, and chickenpox. Some ideas for an exhibit about viruses that you might do include:

- ✦ Viruses—Unseen invaders
- ✦ The common cold—The cause, prevention, treatments
- ✦ A disease caused by a virus, such as rabies, measles, polio, mumps, chickenpox

You grow trillions of microbes in and on your body. A truce has been reached between them and you. Usually, they don't hassle you and you give them food, water, and warmth. However, a defense system is present in your body to repel any invading microbes, or any resident microbes that leave their safe location. It is called the **immune system**. You could prepare an exhibit that features how your body defends against alien microbes:

- ✦ Cell wars—How the body fights invading microbes
- ✦ Immunizations keep us healthy
- ✦ Allergies

Recently, a virus infection has been discovered that eventually destroys part of the immune system. The disease is called AIDS—the initials stand for **A**cquired **I**mmuno**d**eficiency **S**yndrome. People with AIDS die because their immune system cannot handle microbes that healthy people are able to fight off. An exhibit about AIDS that informs people about this dread disease could be made.

Microbes in soil interact with many plants. One thing plants need for growth is nitrogen. They use it to make proteins and vitamins. The roots of some plants are infected with bacteria that convert nitrogen in air into a new substance that the plants can use. The bacteria are said to be **nitrogen-fixing**. Plants that depend on this helpful relationship include soybeans, peas, alfalfa, and clover. They provide food for people and animals. You could prepare an exhibit that explains the importance of nitrogen-fixation in agriculture.

Photos and carefully drawn illustrations are a good idea to include in your exhibit. However, don't tear out pictures from magazines and books. Any written material that you use in this exhibit should be in *your own words*. Your exhibit will be judged, in part, on how creative and original it is.

14

The nodules on the roots of these alfafa plants
contain nitrogen-fixing bacteria.

☞ *Demonstrations*

The library may have some books that describe how to do experiments about something that microbes do or what they look like. Sometimes these are too simple and only take a short time to do. If you decide to do one of these easy projects, it will probably receive a low rating by your teacher or science fair judge.

Here are two ideas for demonstrations about microbes that take a few weeks to complete.

✦ *Make a Winogradsky column*

Microbes live on different diets. These different appetites help microbes recycle substances in nature. If it were not for this recycling, waste would rapidly pile up and smother many living creatures. One building block of natural things is sulfur. You may have noticed a foul odor when you walked past a muddy lake. This smell of rotten eggs is due to a gas called hydrogen sulfide. It has sulfur in it. The gas was made by certain bacteria growing in the mud. Other bacteria can use this gas as food. Some of these bacteria like air and others cannot grow if air is present.

You can observe these different bacteria in a Winogradsky (*WIN oh GRAHD skey*) column. It is named after the Russian microbiologist who studied how bacteria recycle sulfur in nature. Here is how to make a Winogradsky column. You will need a tall glass cylinder. A hydrometer cylinder (38 cm x 375 cm) works well. You might be able to borrow one from a chemistry lab at a local high school or college. They are sold by the biological supply houses listed at the end of this book. For the next step, a responsible adult should help. Get a bucket of wet mud from the edge of a pond or lake and a large jar of water. Use the mud as soon as you get to the place where you will do the work. Weigh about 300 g of mud. Weigh out 3 g of each of these chemicals: calcium sulfate, calcium carbonate, and dipotassium phosphate. Mix these salts with the mud. Next, shred five paper towels and soak the pieces in 100 **milliliters** (ml) of pond or lake water. Add the paper-water mixture to the glass cylinder. Then, pour the mud-salts mixture into the glass cylinder. Use a stick to pack the column so that no air bubbles are visible. You might have to add small amounts of pond water to help release the air bubbles. Add enough mud-salts mixture so that when it finally settles, its level reaches about 75 cm from the cylinder top. Cover the column completely with aluminum foil. (If any water evaporates, add fresh pond water.)

Let the column sit in a dark corner for 2 weeks. Then, remove the foil from the sides. Leave foil on the top of the cylinder. Now, put the column in sunlight for several weeks. Examine the column every three days for changes. You will see sections that are green, brown, or red-purple. Different kinds of bacteria will be living in each section.

✦ Grow "magnetic" bacteria

Bacteria that respond to a magnet grow in muddy waters. These microbes contain crystals that act like a tiny compass. The bacteria apparently swim down along the earth's magnetic field into those parts

Making a Winogradsky column can be messy, but it's fun!

of muck that do not have as much air. Too much oxygen is deadly to these bacteria. See if you can isolate these **magnetotactic** (*mag NET oh TACK tick*) bacteria. Magnetotactic means "attracted to a magnet." You will need several salad dressing-sized jars with screw top lids. Collect mud and water from several places. Ponds and lakes with lots of sediment are good sources. The settling ponds of waste water treatment plants also have been found to have these bacteria. About 25% of the jar should have mud. Water from the same source should fill up the jar to 75% of its volume. When you get the samples home, use several large rubber bands to fasten a flat magnet about halfway up on the outside of each jar. Wrap each jar with aluminum foil. Let the jars sit in a dark corner for two to three weeks. Remove the foil and look for bacteria in the water around the magnet. You may need to use a microscope to see them. A biology teacher may be able to help you prepare a sample to look at under a microscope.

After you read the next section, put on your thinking cap and see if you can add something to a demonstration that will turn it into an investigation.

☞ *Investigations*

The best type of science project shows an investigation that you carried out. By exploring some feature of microbes in an investigation project, you will learn more about how scientists think and work. You will also learn some important things about the world around you.

Let's review again the questions you need to ask as you plan and carry out a project that uses the scientific method:

✔ What do you want to find out? This is the *problem* that you have decided to investigate.

✔ What is already known about the problem?

✔ What is your experimental design for an experiment that will give you an answer to your problem?

✔ What do you think will happen? This is your *hypothesis*.

✔ What did you observe happen? These *observations* are written in your lab notebook.

✔ Analyze your data.

✔ What did you learn from the observations? Did you find that your hypothesis was correct? If not, can you think of another hypothesis? These are your *conclusions.*

Here are some suggestions for an investigation you could do about microbes.

✦ *Yeasts and fermentation*

Yeasts eat sugar for energy and to make more yeast cells. When they finish dining on the sugar, yeast cells "burp" and release the gas carbon dioxide. They also spit out alcohol. The name for this process is **fermentation**.

You can measure how much carbon dioxide bubbles out of yeast cells by an easy method. Three packets of dried yeast are dissolved in 225 ml of warm water. Then, 125 ml of corn syrup (or other food) and 75 ml of yeast solution are mixed in a clean glass. The solution is then carefully poured through a funnel into a glass soda pop bottle. A large balloon is slipped over the opening in the bottle. A string or rubber band is fastened around the balloon where it fits over the bottle's neck. The bottle is then laid on its side in a warm place (30°C or 86°F). In about 30 to 45 minutes, you should see bubbles in the solution. The bubbles are carbon dioxide. Their appearance shows that fermentation is taking place.

Yeasts can blow up a balloon.

You could design an experiment that investigates possible foods for yeast to ferment. These might include table sugar, other sugars like lactose and maltose (available at health food stores), fruit juices, flour, plain gelatin, and oils. You can compare how much carbon dioxide is made in different bottles by measuring the diameter of each balloon.

You could also find out what chemicals are harmful to yeast. Some chemicals you could investigate are bleach, ammonia, liquid cleaner, detergent, rubbing alcohol, vinegar, antiseptics, and tea. A responsible adult should help with these. Add 50 ml of a chemical to a soda pop bottle that has a mixture of yeast and corn syrup. Compare the results to a bottle without the chemical

✦ *Soil microbes and plants*

Many different microbes live in the soil. Some bacteria turn substances in the earth into **nutrients**, or food, that plants can use to grow. Many of these helpful microbes live right next to plant roots where these nutrients can be absorbed.

You could see how necessary these soil bacteria are to plant growth. Transplant corn, wheat, tomato, bean, or pine seedlings into pots containing different soils. Use soil taken from a garden, soil that has been sterilized by heating in the oven, and soil that has been shaken from older plants. Compare heights after six or seven weeks. Organic garden supply companies sell bacterial additives. You could see if they really work!

✦ *Tooth brushing and dental plaque*

You know that brushing your teeth is important to prevent tooth decay. But do you know why? Certain bacteria that grow on your teeth are the problem. They are called *Streptococcus mutans* (*STREHP toe COCK cuss mew TANS*). They look like a chain of beads on a necklace when they are observed in a microscope. These bacteria use the table sugar you eat for food. They use some of it to make a sticky substance that helps them stay attached to your teeth. But, they don't get washed away when you drink or chew. Over time, this stuff forms **plaque**. Unfortunately, these bacteria also ooze out an acid made from the sugar. This acid weakens tooth enamel, which is usually very hard. The softened enamel begins to flake off. Other bacteria can now start to eat tooth material under the enamel. This spot grows into a cavity. Plaque is removed by brushing your teeth.

You could learn how effective tooth brushing is by observing the variety and number of bacteria scraped off your teeth. Bacteria can be sampled by wiping teeth with a sterile cotton swab. The bacteria on swab are then spread on the surface of nutrient agar (*AH gar*) in a plastic Petri dish. Agar is a jelly-like material extracted from seaweed. Most bacteria cannot eat agar. Food for the bacteria is dissolved in the agar.

Place the dishes in a warm, dark place for several days. Examine the plate for growth of bacteria. **Colonies**, visible accumulations of bacteria, will be scattered over the agar surface. Each colony represents a single bacterium cell that came off the cotton swab. Look for colonies with different shapes and colors. Avoid opening the plates. You can buy material for culturing bacteria from one of the biological supply houses listed at the end of the book.

You could also investigate if different toothpaste brands work better to remove plaque, or if mouthwashes really get rid of plaque.

This is what bacterial colonies look like as they grow on the surface of agar in a Petri plate.

✦ *Deodorants and skin bacteria*

Your skin nourishes many bacteria. These bacteria break down oils that come out of sweat glands, forming smelly chemicals. Wet areas of the body, like under your arms or your feet, harbor lots of these odor-causing bacteria. Advertisements for some soaps and underarm deodorants state that they kill these bacteria.

You could find out if these claims are correct. See if washing or spraying with these products after you have not bathed for one or two

21

days really reduces the number of bacteria under your arms and between your toes. You can see the bacteria when you use the steps described above for growing bacteria from teeth.

✦ *Microbes make things biodegradable*

Earlier in this book you read how microbes in soil break down dead plant and animal matter. This process of decay changes organic material into nutrients that other organisms can use for growth. Materials that microbes can rot are said to be **biodegradable**.

You could design an experiment that looks at bacteria growing in soils which decay biodegradable substances. Cut the top half from four plastic one-gallon jugs. *Be careful not to cut yourself with a sharp knife or scissors*. Fill each with soil taken from a damp place in a woods or from under a rotting log. Choose some things that you think are biodegradable. These might include cloth, leaves, newspaper, orange peel, and cardboard. Prepare four samples of each item. Bury one of each sample in a different plastic jug filled with soil. Cover the jugs so they don't dry out and place them in a warm, dark corner. Keep the soil very damp, but not sopping wet.

After one week, dig out the objects from one jug. Examine them to see if they have started to decay. Use a sterile cotton swab to remove a little of the soil and material from each sample. Prepare a stained microscope slide of each sample and look at it with the microscope. Record your observations. Use another sterile cotton swab to spread a little more of the same material over a nutrient agar in a Petri dish. Place the dishes in a warm, dark corner for several days. Examine the dishes for growth of microbes.

After two, three, and four weeks, repeat this procedure with the other jugs. Do you see any differences in the microbes as time goes on?

Another experiment could examine how different soils and the microbes growing in them affect the decay of the same objects. You could collect sandy soil, soil from a bog, or soil that has lots of clay. Do the same experiments and compare the results.

These science projects allow you to make predictions, something scientists want to do with the data they have collected. What is *most* important about the project you choose is that you are curious about it and involved with it.

CHAPTER 3
Planning Your Project

Stating your purpose

When you have finally picked a problem to study about microbes, you then need to state the purpose of the investigation that you want to do. You can either make a statement or ask a question For example:

"The purpose of this experiment is to determine if deodorant soaps and underarm deodorants affect the number of bacteria that grow on the body."

or

"Do deodorant soaps and underarm deodorants affect the number of bacteria that grow on the body?"

Notice that each of these sentences clearly states what the experimenter wants to find out. You should take some time to write a sentence that defines the problem you have decided to tackle. This will help make clear what you want to do during your investigation. The statement of your problem will be written in your *lab notebook*. Later in this chapter, you will learn more about this notebook and the "stuff" you should keep in it.

Gathering information for your project

☞ *The library*

The first place you want to visit to find information for your project is the library. This is where you will find books, encyclopedias, magazines, and newspapers with articles about microbes.

The card or on-line computer catalog will tell you what books the library has. Look up the subject headings "Medicine," "Microbiology,"

"Bacteria," "Fungi," "Viruses," and "Science Experiments."

To find magazine articles about microbes, use the *Readers' Guide to Periodical Literature.* There is a volume for each year. Look up the topics "Bacteria," "Viruses," or "Fungi." For each article you will find the magazine's name, the volume number, and the pages on which the article appears. Ask the librarian for help if you need it.

Scientists use libraries a lot to find out what is going on in their area of interest. So this library search is good experience for a young scientist.

As you read, it is important that you take good notes. Index cards (3 x 5 inches) work well. Don't write on scraps of paper. They are easily lost. Write down information that will help you organize your ideas and to plan the steps you will take to do your project. Each index card should include the author's name (if any); the name of the book, magazine, or newspaper; the date it was published; and the pages you read. Later, you will rewrite important index card information into your lab notebook.

Writing out note cards is a smart thing to do.

Use your own words when you summarize what a book or an article says. **Plagiarism**, that is, copying word-for-word, or changing just a few words here and there, is not proper behavior for any scientist. Teachers and science fair judges will not accept it. What you write on your display and in your report about your project *must be in your own words*.

☞ *Resource people*

Your community probably has several people who can give you some help on your project about microbes. They include nurses, dentists, doctors, and pharmacists. Hospital laboratories employ people who spend their time finding out what microbes are causing people to be sick. Talk with personnel at a waste water treatment plant or at a landfill. Perhaps there is a college nearby where you will find a helpful biology professor. You might talk this scientist into giving you some bacteria and other materials for doing your project.

Don't hesitate to get all of the information you can. The more you know, the better your project will be.

Scientists are easy to talk to.

How an investigation is done

☞ *Experimental design*

Once you have decided *what* you want to find out about microbes, the next step is to decide *how* you will do it. You must decide what materials you need to use and what you will do with them. This is called the **experimental design**. In a scientific investigation, the answers to your problem should come from the experiments you plan.

A well-designed science project that investigates a problem about microbes is often done under **controlled conditions**. This means that you intentionally change certain conditions to see how the specific feature of a microbe you are examining changes. The conditions of an experiment that change are called the **variables**. You change the **independent variable** to see how the **dependent variable** changes. Here's another way of explaining these variables. The independent variable is something that you change on purpose. The variable that responds to this change is the dependent variable.

This may still be a little confusing. So, let's see how these terms apply to the experiment about rotting wood that was described in Chapter 1. In this experiment, different wood samples are placed in soil for several weeks. Then the amount of wood that has been eaten by soil microbes is measured. An independent variable (a variable that is changed on purpose) is the type of wood—pine, redwood, or fir. A dependent variable (a variable that responds to the change) is the percentage of wood that has rotted away. The different wood blocks are called the **experimental groups**.

Control groups are also needed in an experiment. In the experiment on rotting wood, one of the jars contains just wood blocks—there is no soil. The wood blocks in this control jar should show no decrease in weight. They were exposed to the same conditions as were the wood blocks stuck in soil, except they were not set in soil. Another control jar could contain soil that has been heated to 160°C (320°F) for 2 hours to kill any microbes. This would show that the soil must contain living things for decay to happen.

An experiment must have results that are repeatable. This means that if you do the experiment again, you get the same results that you obtained the first time. If you have time, it is a good idea to repeat the experiment two or three times.

Ask your teacher, parent, or other knowledgeable adult to check over your design. Let them make changes that might make the experiments safer or easier to do. However, make sure that the plan is *your* plan.

☞ *Lab Notebook*

You will need a lab notebook in which to write down everything about your experiment. This includes what you want to find out and what your hypothesis is for the outcome of the experiment. The notebook also contains a list of the materials you use and how they are used. You record what you observe or measure. You could include photographs you take of your project. You write down what you think the data you collected means. You list all of the sources you used to gather information to help you in the project. This includes people, books, and magazines. The first page will have the project's title, followed by your name, grade, and school. A table of contents at the beginning will help readers find the different parts of the project.

The lab notebook could be a spiral-bound notebook or a three-ring binder. It should be used only for your science project. Remember to write everything down in this book—don't use scraps of paper. The notebook does not have to be real neat, but your handwriting should be clear enough so other people can read your ideas. Your teacher and science fair judges will look at it.

☞ *Materials*

The things that you will use for your project on microbes must be chosen with care. The list of materials must be *exact*. It states *what* and *how much* will be needed to do the project.

You should have little problem finding materials to be used in your project on microbes. In the section that gives project ideas, some materials for doing experiments are identified. Other sources are listed at the end of this book. If you want to buy something from a biological supply company, ask your teacher or other adult to place the order. Remember that it may take several weeks for the order to reach you, so begin to plan your work early.

☞ *Procedures*

The steps that you will follow in your experiment must be carefully organized. As you think about how you will do your experiment, write down each of the steps in the order they will be done. Include as much detail as possible. Your experimental design, or plan, should be written in your lab notebook.

A **flow chart** will help to remind you of the various steps that you need to follow in your experiments. This chart is a simple version of your experimental design. It reminds you what must be done next. Check off each step as you complete it.

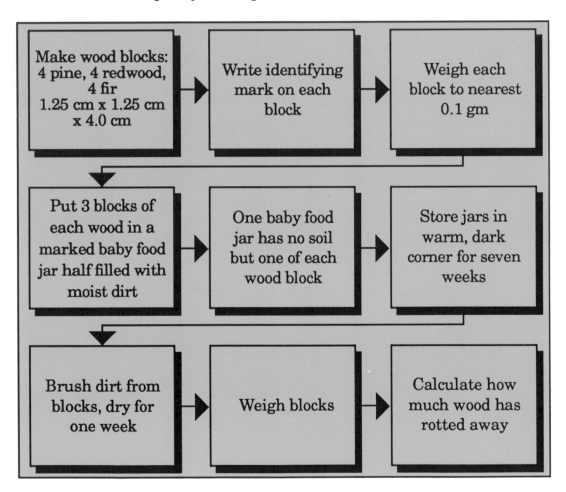

This is a flow chart for the experiment on rotting wood.

☞ *Measure in Metrics*

All of your measurements should use the metric system. Scientists all over the world measure length, volume, mass, and temperature in metric units. Measuring in metrics is easy because it is based on the number 10. This is just like American money. One dollar can be divided into 10 dimes or 100 pennies. In the metric system, you will not have to worry about fractions. You will use decimals.

The basic metric unit for length is the **meter** (m). One meter is a little longer than one yard. A 100 yard football field measures 91.5 m. A meter is divided into 100 equal and smaller units called **centimeters** (cm). A meter is divided into 1000 equal and still smaller units called **millimeters** (mm). Most rulers will have the metric scale printed on one side.

The basic metric unit of volume is the **liter** (l). One liter of lemonade is a little larger than one quart. A liter is divided into 1000 equal and smaller units called **milliliters** (ml). A 12 ounce can of soda pop holds 296 ml. Measuring cups and medicine droppers can be used to measure amounts of liquids in milliliters. Your school might have graduated cylinders for measuring liquids.

The basic metric unit of **mass** is the **gram** (g). Mass measures the amount of matter, or "stuff," present in an object. Many people confuse mass with weight. Mass is not influenced by gravity as weight is. Large objects have their mass measured in **kilograms** (kg). A kilogram equals 1000 g. Some electronic kitchen scales will measure grams.

Temperature in the metric system is measured in degrees Celsius (°C). People who give the weather forecast on TV use the Fahrenheit (°F) scale. Water freezes at 0°C, or 32°F, and boils at 100°C, or 212°F. Body temperature is 37°C, or 98.6°F. A thermometer on a nice spring day might read 25°C, or 77°F.

Metric System Symbols

Length	Volume	Mass
meter = m	liter = l	gram = g
centimeter = cm	milliliter = ml	kilogram = kg
millimeter = mm		

☞ *Time schedule*

You should begin to plan your project several months before it is due. This will give you enough time to gather materials, do the project work, analyze the information you gather, write a report, and prepare a display. Estimate how much time each step should take and then add a little more time.

Here is a sample time schedule for an investigative project:

Week 1	- Choose a problem
Weeks 2 and 3	- Gather information
Weeks 4 and 5	- Plan your experiment and gather your materials
Week 6	- Begin your experiment
Week 7	- Continue to collect data from your experiment
Week 8	- Finish data collection; begin to analyze data
Week 9	- Prepare graphs; make display
Week 10	- Practice oral report; science fair starts or project is due

You will have fewer hassles if you carefully plan a time schedule. This will help make sure that your project is finished in plenty of time for the science fair.

CHAPTER 4

Doing Your Project

Safety

"Safety first!" is the rule when working on a science project. Here are some tips to keep you from possibly becoming ill or being injured.

A responsible adult, such as your teacher, the school nurse, or a scientist who is familiar with microbes, should check your project plan for possible dangers. Any work with bacteria or molds grown on nutrient agar is best done with the help of a science teacher, or other adult, who has experience with microbes.

Even though the microbes you may grow are probably harmless, act as if they could make you sick. Wash your hands thoroughly with soap and water each time you finish handling any material. Don't touch any colonies of microbes. Keep your hands away from your eyes, nose, and mouth while you are working with any experimental material. Don't drink, eat, or even put gum in your mouth until you have washed your hands.

If you have diabetes, leukemia or an illness caused by a faulty immune system, ask your family doctor if it is OK for you to work with microbes. If you want to work at home and someone in your family has one of these illnesses, check with your doctor for approval.

Have a place of your own to work on your project. It might be a table in your classroom that your teacher assigns to you. A corner of the basement, the garage, or your room at home can also be used. Don't grow any microbes where food is prepared or eaten. You will need a desk to write on. Keep your work area neat. As you do your project, be sure to clean up. Put away things that you no longer need. Wipe off your work area with a household disinfectant each time you finish your work. If you spill anything that contains growing microbes, disinfect it *before* you wipe it up. When your experiments are completed, place any materials that have microbes growing on them in a bag and put it in the trash. Things growing in water can be flushed down the toilet.

31

If any chemicals are used in your project, use them *only* with an adult to supervise you. Wear protective glasses, rubber gloves, and a rubber apron. Wash your hands each time you finish using the chemicals. Keep your hands away from your mouth while you work. All chemicals should be clearly labelled and stored in a safe container.

Any electrical equipment should use batteries to power it. Electricity from a wall socket is too dangerous to use. Even though the current from batteries is not strong, wires coming from them can become hot and cause a burn.

Avoid using sharp objects that could puncture the skin.

Most science fair rules don't allow live microbes in your project display. Check the rules carefully.

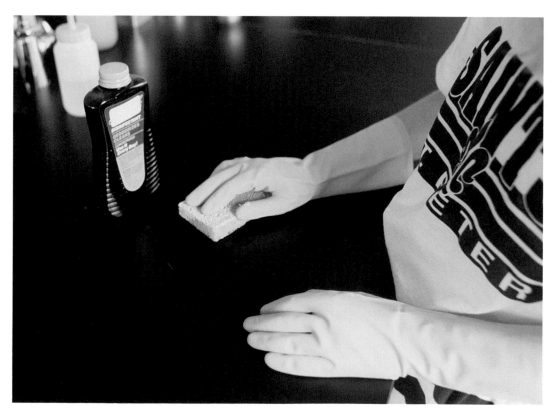

Remember: "Safety first" when you do your project.

Keeping a record

The lab notebook in which you wrote background information is also used to record your observations of the experiment. You can't write down too much! Don't expect to remember later what you saw or measured. Write down your measurements and observations *right away*!

There are two kinds of observations that you can record. A **qualitative** observation does not use measurements: "The balloon inflated by yeast grown on maltose sugar was smaller than the balloon inflated by yeast grown on sucrose." A **quantitative** observation uses measurements and numbers: "The diameter of the balloon inflated with gas released by yeast grown with table sugar was 25 mm less than the diameter of the balloon inflated with gas released by yeast grown with maltose sugar." Quantitative observations are more *precise*. Whenever possible, use quantitative observations for your project.

A scientist must be **unbiased** when observing what happens in the experiment. This means that you don't make the results come out the way you want them to. If the results are not turning out as you predicted, that's OK. Maybe your hypothesis is not correct. That's OK, too. An incorrect hypothesis means that you can rule out your "educated guess" as a possibility. Honesty is expected of scientists.

When you compare measurements of different groups, you will want to figure an average measurement for the subjects in each group. An average is a way to represent the measurements for all subjects within a group. The arithmetic you use to compute an average is simple to do. Let's suppose that you are measuring the diameters of three balloons inflated by gas released by yeast growing in molasses. These diameters are added together. The sum is then divided by the number of subjects in this experimental group. The answer from this last calculation is the average measurement for the group.

135 mm	141 mm	The average diameter of a
148 mm	3 ⟌ 423	balloon blown up by yeast
+140 mm	3	growing in table sugar
423 mm	12	is **141 mm.**
	12	
	3	
	3	

Photos that show you working on different parts of your investigation are one way to keep a record of your observations. These pictures should be clear. Make sure that your subjects are well-lighted. Hand-drawn illustrations that are neat can also be used.

Coming to conclusions

When you have completed your experiments, it is time to come to some conclusions. You did the experiment to get an answer to a question. Did your observations support your hypothesis? Explain everything in your lab notebook. If your data don't support your hypothesis, don't worry. Avoid stating that the experiment was a "failure", or that it didn't work. Just explain what happened. Maybe some variable was not controlled. Go back over your notes in the lab notebook to find out where a mistake might have been made.

The most important conclusion is a statement of what your experiment means. For example, "Pine rots much faster than does redwood. This means that pine is not a good choice of wood to use when a deck is built." Thus, your conclusions tie together what you found out from your experiment with the world in which you live.

Redwood or cedar are good choices for building a deck.

CHAPTER 5

Presenting Your Project

Making graphs to show your data

Numbers you collected from your observations can be formed into **graphs**. Graphs will pack lots of information into a little space. They are a good way to present your data because they make it easier to understand the information. Paper on which to draw graphs can be bought at office supply departments. It comes with lines printed on the sheet. Use graph paper that has four or five lines per inch.

A **bar graph** can be made when you want to compare several groups. Bars may be drawn to represent the average amount measured for each group. A bar graph would be used to compare the groups. To see how a bar graph can be made, let's use some data collected from an experiment. It shows the number of bacterial colonies that grew on agar before and after washing under the arms with two deodorant soaps.

When underarms sampled	Number of bacterial colonies
Before washing	172
After washing with Soap A	56
After washing with Soap B	132

A line (the **horizontal axis**) is drawn at the bottom of the graph. This baseline has a place for each group. This line represents the independent variables, or the variables that you change on purpose. For our example, the independent variable is the soap used. The line on the graph's left side (the **vertical axis**) displays the amount of each dependent variable. This is the measurement that changes in response to the change you cause. The number of bacterial colonies that grew is the dependent variable in our example.

Drawing a bar graph to show your data takes careful planning. A bar's height is proportional to an amount. Thus, you must decide how high each bar will be drawn on the graph paper. In our example, one cm on the graph paper represents 10 colonies. Choose how wide the bars will be—the bar widths must be the same. The bars can be drawn in different colors to make each group stand out.

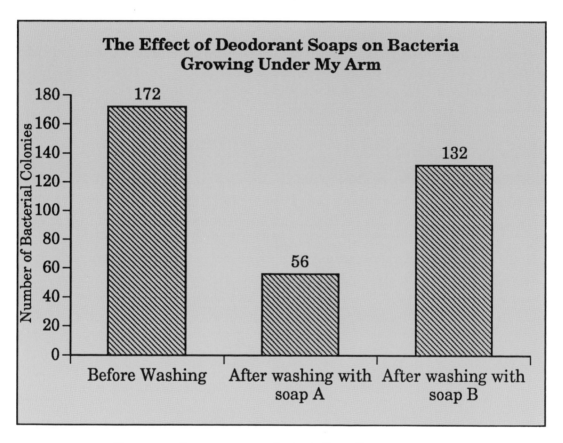

Bar graphs compare data taken from groups.

A **pictograph** is constructed like a bar graph except that it uses a repeating symbol to represent the amount of an item. If there is a fraction in this amount, only a part of the symbol is used. The symbol you choose to use should have a simple shape that readers can easily recognize. As for a bar graph, you should plan a pictograph's layout. Decide how many symbols will need to appear in each row. You will use many copies of this symbol. So, all symbols in the pictograph must look the same. There are several ways to do this. You could carefully draw your design and then make many copies on a copy machine. You could, instead, cut out your symbol from a piece of cardboard and then trace around the design.

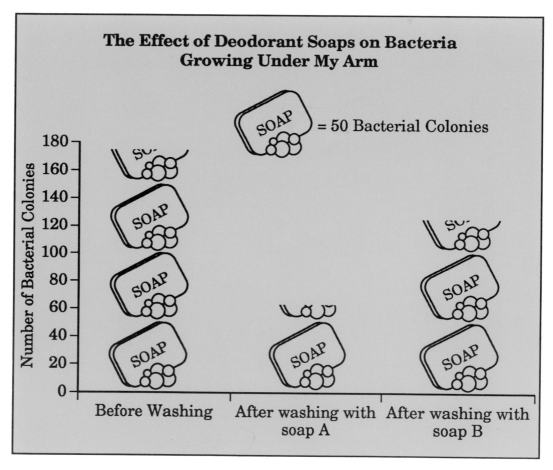

Pictographs are a type of bar graph.

A **line graph** uses a continuous line to show how the dependent variable in an experiment changes as the independent variable is changed. Frequently, a line graph shows how an experimental group changes over time. In these situations, time (minutes, days, weeks) is the independent variable, and so it is plotted along the horizontal axis. The dependent variable (the amount of change) is on the vertical axis.

If you prepare a line graph that compares data taken from different experimental groups, the line for each group can be a different color.

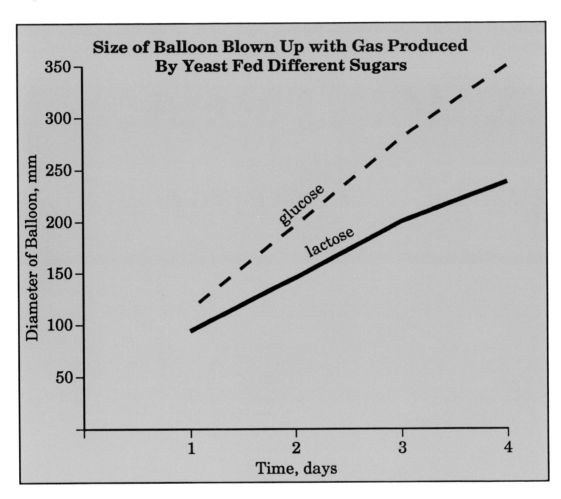

Line graphs show a change over time.

All graphs must have labels on the left side and at the bottom. These labels are written so that the reader will know what the numbers represent. In addition, each graph must have a title that tells what observations are being shown.

Lettering in a graph must be neat. You can use press-on letters purchased from an office supply store. Letters can also be traced using a template. If you have access to a computer, it can be used to prepare a graph with proper labels.

Putting your display together

Visitors to your science project must be able to understand quickly what your project is about and what you did. A science project display tells a short story of your work on the project. It should show:

> ☆ A statement of the problem—what you wanted to find out.
>
> ☆ The hypothesis—how you guessed the experiment might turn out.
>
> ☆ Materials and methods—what materials you used and what you did with them.
>
> ☆ The results—what you observed.
>
> ☆ Your conclusions—did you find out what you wanted to know?

Science fairs usually have rules on the basic design of a display. Check with your teacher for local regulations, especially on the size of the space made available for you to show your project.

The most common display has three panels and stands by itself. Several sturdy materials are available for these panels. Panels can be made of ¼ or ⅜ inch plywood held together with hinges. The plywood can be painted or covered with cloth or paper. Foam board is lightweight, but strong enough to hold your written materials. Panels are easily cut out with a knife. Cloth tape can be used to make hinges that hold panels together. Foam board is available at office supply stores. Pegboard is also a handy material to use. It has holes already in it for hanging items. Because pegboard may bend if heavy objects are attached, you can nail 1" x 2" wood strips around the edges of the pegboard. Once these wood strips have been nailed on, hinges can be added. Some office supply stores and biological supply companies sell cardboard displays.

The center panel shows the project's title and some of the graphs you made from the data. Pictures of the experimental setup could be placed here also. On the left side, the statement of the problem and your hypothesis are shown. The right side can display any other results, as well as your conclusions. Each of these items is written or typed on a separate piece of paper.

Letters for the title can be cut from construction paper and should be at least two inches high. While neat hand printing is OK, your display will look better if you use a typewriter or computer for the other lettering. Since visitors to your display will stand several feet away, letters should be at least ¼ inch high. Be sure to have someone check the spelling, grammar, and punctuation in your display before you put it all together.

You will want to include drawings or photographs to help explain your experiment. These illustrations must be clearly labelled. Science fair rules forbid harmful live bacteria as part of your project display. Even if your microbes are considered harmless, play it safe—don't bring them along as part of your display.

How you attach materials to the display board is important. Staples look cheap! Tape hidden behind larger pieces works well. Test any glues you might use to find one that does not wrinkle paper after it dries. Before you fasten the pieces in place, lay everything out to see how it will look and fit on the display board.

Making a neat display is important.

Your written report

In addition to the lab notebook that was discussed in Chapters 3 and 4, some science fairs will expect that you prepare a written report on your project. This formally presents your work on the project. It shows readers the details of your efforts.

If possible, use a typewriter or computer. However, *very* neat handwriting is acceptable. The pages can be bound into a folder or a binder.

On the first page is the title of the project, your name, grade, and school. The table of contents is the second page. Readers can more easily find different sections if they know what pages to look up. The

Microbes and
Rotting of Wood

Paul Biederman
Grade 5
Eisenhower School
Middletown, Florida

Table of Contents

statement of the problem explains why you wanted to work on this project about microbes and what you wanted to find out about them. Included in the background research section are summaries of the articles and books you may have read (remember to use the note cards you made), the names and titles of the people to whom you may have talked and what you learned from them, and any other materials you found to help you plan your project. This is followed by your hypothesis and your plan to test it.

The materials you used, how you used them, what data you obtained, and what the data mean are the next sections. The information you should include in these sections has been discussed earlier in this book.

The bibliography lists all articles and books you read. These materials are listed alphabetically by the authors' last names. Here are some examples to help you prepare a bibliography:

For a magazine:
Barinaga, Marcia. "The secret of saltiness." Science 254:664-665 (1991).

For a book:
Hodges, Laurent. Environmental pollution. New York: Holt, Rinehart and Winston, 1977.

Finally, you need to acknowledge all of those people who helped you on the project. Those who gave you the greatest support and help should be listed first.

Judging of your project

You will probably be expected to talk about your project to science fair judges or to your class. In four or five minutes you will have to:

- Introduce yourself, giving your name, school, and grade.
- Give the title of your project.
- Give the purpose of your project.
- Tell why you choose this project.
- Explain what you did.
- Show your results—explain any graphs or pictures that are in your display.
- Give your conclusions if you did an investigation project.
- Explain what you learned.
- Ask if there are any questions.

You can use notes to help remind you of what to say. However, if you practice several times, you won't have to look at them too often. Practice your talk while a parent, other relative, or a teacher listens. Ask this person for helpful suggestions.

When you finally give your talk, stand to the side of your display so the judge or other viewers can see your work. Talk slowly, even if you are really nervous! If you don't know the answer to a question, be sure to say you don't know. Remember, honesty is important.

The science fair judges who visit with at your display will score your project for an award. Each science fair usually prepares its own judging sheet. However, most will score projects in these areas:

✔ Scientific thought - The judges will see if your project follows the scientific method. Has the problem been clearly stated? Are the procedures proper and thorough? Have controls been properly used?

✔ Creative ability - The judges will want to know how you chose this topic. Your score will be lower if you repeated something you read in a book or if someone else did the actual work. If a book, like this one, gave you the idea for your project, did you use your imagination to develop the project more fully? More points will usually be given for scientific thought and for creativity than for the other areas.

✔ Understanding - Judges will ask some questions to see if you understand the key scientific features of your project. If you have prepared an exhibit, does the display provide some answers to questions about the topic?

✔ Clarity - The judges will examine your project to see if it clearly presents the hypothesis, procedures, data, and conclusions. Will the average person understand the project?

✔ Technical skill - Finally, the judges will check on how your display appears. How attractive is your display? Did you carefully check written materials for correct spelling and grammar?

Final words of encouragement

When you have presented your science fair project to your family, friends, and judges, feel good about what you have done. You have worked hard. You have become more aware of what scientists do. You have learned how to find answers to a question about microbes. By doing this project, you have discovered more of the wonder of science. Get fired-up and do another science fair project next year!

WHERE YOU CAN BUY SUPPLIES FOR EXPERIMENTS ABOUT MICROBES

Carolina Biological Supply Co.
2700 York Road
Burlington, NC 27215
1-800-334-5551 (East of the Rockies)
1-800-547-1733 (Rockies and West)
1-800-632-1231 (North Carolina)

Connecticut Valley Biological Supply Co., Inc.
P.O. Box 326
Southampton, MA 01073
1-800-628-7748 (U.S.)
1-800-282-7757 (Mass.)

Nasco
P.O. Box 901
Fort Atkinson, WI 53538-0901
1-800-558-9595

Science Kit & Boreal Laboratories
777 East Park Drive
Tonawanda, NY 14150-6784
OR
P.O. Box 2726
Santa Fe Springs, CA 90670-4490
1-800-828-7777

Ward's
P.O. Box 92912
Rochester, NY 14692-9012
1-800-962-2660

GLOSSARY

antibiotic - a substance made by microbes that stops bacteria from growing or that kills bacteria.

bacilli (singular, **bacillus**) - bacteria that look like rice grains or short sticks when they are viewed in a microscope.

bacteria (singular, **bacterium**) - microscopic primitive living things that live everywhere on Earth.

bar graph - a graph that uses columns to compare different values obtained for experimental groups. The height of each bar is proportional to the value.

binary fission - the way bacteria reproduce: 1 cell divides to form 2 new identical cells.

biodegradable - capable of being broken down, or eaten by microbes.

centimeter - the distance measured by 1/100 (0.01) meter. There are 2.54 centimeters in one inch (abbreviation: cm).

cocci (singular, **coccus**) - bacteria that look like tiny balls when they are viewed in a microscope.

colony - visible growth of bacteria on the surface of agar. The billions of cells in a colony are the offspring of a single cell that was deposited on the agar.

conclusions - what you interpret the results of an experiment to mean.

control group - a group in an experiment in which as many variables as possible are kept constant because they could affect the outcome of the experiment.

data - the observations and measurements that you make in an experiment.

dependent variable - the factor or condition that changes as a result of the presence of, or a deliberate change you make in, the independent variable.

enzyme - a substance that living things use to change chemicals.

experimental design - the plans you make so you can do an experiment. The design includes what you will use and how you intend to use them.

experimental group - a group in which all variables are the same as those in the control group *except* for the factor that you are following in your experiment.

fermentation - a process in which yeasts release gas and alcohol after they have finished eating sugar.

flow chart - a list that is a shortened version of the steps you want to follow in doing your experiment. As you complete each step, you should check it off the list.

fungi - microbes that live on dead things. Like bacteria, fungi are primary causes of rot.

gram - the basic unit of mass in the metric system. There are 28.3 grams in one ounce (abbreviation: g).

hypothesis - a statement that gives a possible answer to a question. Because you may already know something about the question, a hypothesis is sometimes called an "educated guess." To see if it is true or not, a hypothesis is tested by doing an experiment.

horizontal axis - the line on a graph that goes across the bottom. It is used for showing values for the independent variable.

immune system - the body's defense against microbes that try to live in and on the body.

independent variable - the factor or condition that you want to study. In an experiment, you intentionally change this factor.

kilogram - the mass of 1000 grams. One kilogram is equivalent to about 2.2 pounds (abbreviation: kg).

line graph - a graph that uses a line to show how the dependent variable changes as the independent variable is changed.

liter - the basic unit of volume in the metric system. One liter is a little smaller than one quart (abbreviation: l).

magnetotactic bacteria - bacteria that have iron crystals inside them, which cause the bacteria to move in the Earth's magnetic field like tiny compasses.

mass - the amount of matter, or "stuff," that is present. Weight is often confused with mass. Weight is the pulling force of gravity on matter.

meter - the basic unit of length in the metric system. One meter is a little longer (39.4 inches) than one yard (abbreviation: m).

microbes - living things that must be greatly magnified to be seen. They include bacteria, fungi, and viruses.

milliliter - 1/1000 (one one-thousandths) of a liter. There are approximately 28 milliliters in one fluid ounce (abbreviation: ml).

millimeter - 1/1000 (one one-thousandths) of a meter. There are approximately 25 millimeters in one inch (abbreviation: mm).

molds - fungi that look like fuzzy masses as they grow on fruit, cheese, or bread.

nitrogen-fixation - the process in which chemical factories in bacteria convert nitrogen in the air into organic substances.

nutrients - another word for food.

organic matter - substances made by living things.

pictograph - a graph that uses a series of pictures to show the values measured or observed for the dependent variables. It is put together like a bar graph.

plagiarism - copying word-for-word what someone else has written and not giving credit to that person.

plaque - sticky layer made by bacteria growing on teeth from sugar. Too much plaque can lead to cavities in teeth.

prediction - what you think will happen in an experiment.

qualitative observation - an outcome of an experiment that is not an amount that can be measured, such as color.

quantitative observation - an outcome of an experiment that is measurable, such as numbers of individuals.

results - what you measure or observe as an experiment is carried out.

scientific method - a systematic strategy scientists use to discover answers to questions about the world. It includes making a hypothesis, testing the hypothesis with experiments, collecting and analyzing the results, and arriving at a conclusion.

spore - a round structure made by some fungi for reproducing themselves.

sterilize - to kill all living things, especially microbes, in or on something.

unbiased - not allowing your preferences to interfere with collecting or analyzing data in an experiment.

variable - some factor in an experiment that can be changed.

vertical axis - the line on the left side of a graph. It shows the values of the dependent variables.

yeast - a fungus that looks like a football when viewed in a microscope. Yeasts frequently grow where sugar is easily available, such as on fruit and flowers.

INDEX